One Hand Clapping

Also published by Gerda Hoover:

Private Moments, a book of poetry reflecting on life, death, grief, separation, faith and healing which included whimsical observations of animals.

Comments about *Private Moments:*

"*Private Moments* is a collection of 46 poems, each revealing emotions about life and death, love and heartbreak, and sadness and joy. Some allude to rebirth and a renewed spirit."
—Jane Charmelo
The Lombardian

"My congratulations to you for such an accomplishment. Your poetry was delightful to read."
—Roger K. Miller
Superintendent,
District 86, Hinsdale

One Hand Clapping

Love, Loss, and Beyond

Gerda Hoover

VANTAGE PRESS
New York

FIRST EDITION

All rights reserved, including the right of
reproduction in whole or in part in any form.

Copyright © 2005 by Gerda Hoover

Published by Vantage Press, Inc.
419 Park Ave. South, New York, NY 10016

Manufactured in the United States of America
ISBN: 0-533-15143-0

Library of Congress Catalog Card No.: 2004195727

0 9 8 7 6 5 4 3 2 1

In memory of my husband
who was the love of my life

Contents

Foreword   xi
Acknowledgments   xiii

Earlier Years	1
Later Years	2
"Dusty"	3
A Happy Anniversary	5
You, My Heart	6
In the Blink of an Eye	7
Loss	8
What Next?	9
Mortally Wounded	10
Be Strong	11
Hurting Still	12
Wondering	13
Day after Day	14
View from the Kitchen Window	15
One Hand Clapping	16
I Want to Live Again	17
Moments Remembered	18
I Sold Your Car	19
Yearning	20
I Walk Alone	21
Life Goes On	22
How Do I Miss You	23
The Way We Were	24

Lived, Loved, Lost	25
Never to Know Each Other	26
Am I Really Old Now?	27
Senseless Hurts	28
Let's Not Do It!	29
Answers, Please!	30
Man Buying Flowers	31
To Be Loved Again	32
An Unexpected Friend	33
Invitation to a Party	34
The Empty Chair	36
What Did You Love?	37
Guidelines for Life	38
One Last Kiss	39
First Christmas without You, My Love	40
The Nutty Squirrel	41
The Christmas Tree	42
A Summer's Eve Remembered	43
Pure As the Driven Snow	44
Beyond	45
Hard Dates without You	46
My Sweetheart	47
Night into Morning	48
A Very Special Bracelet	49
Cat's "Happy Birthday" to a Dear Friend	50
North to South	51
"Life Is But a Dream"	53
Sunday	54
Rubber Bands	55
Then and Now	56
My Love	58
Not for Me	60
Imperfect Joy	61
Wishing	62

Be Careful What You Pray For! A Very Short Story	63
When Breaks Happen	65
Traveling Alone	66
Autumn Dance of the Leaves	67
How Tall You Have Grown	68
Love's Power	69
Carpe Diem	70

Foreword

In *One Hand Clapping: Love, Loss, and Beyond,* Gerda Hoover expresses private yet universally shared experiences with deep feelings. She evokes varied emotions. Having lived in a long and happy marriage, the author faces the sudden and unexpected death of her husband. She pours her grief into poems and slowly struggles toward accepting and affirming life as a widow. Nature still holds special moments and touching experiences for her which find their way into charming and moving poetry. The author shows she can still find life worth living.

Gerda Hoover's poetry is inspiring and can encourage people and give them hope.

—Christy Waltersdorff
Pastor, York Center Church of the Brethren
Lombard, Illinois

Acknowledgments

I am deeply grateful to the following people who encouraged, inspired and supported me:

Michael Evans, Ph.D., therapist and teacher
Janice Holley, artistic designer
Franz Langhammer, professor emeritus of German
Tom Mullen, author and lecturer
Christy Waltersdorff, pastor
Darwin Walton, author

Special thanks go further to my loyal friends who assisted me with fine-tuning my writing and helped me heal:

Gail Avgeris
George Batek
Stephanie Erickson
Diana Filippi
Carol Stack

One Hand Clapping

Earlier Years

World War II was over.
He was the first American
to study at the University of Hamburg
where I was a student
A friend introduced me to him
We dated
We fell in love
but a semester is so short,
and he needed to study another semester
at the University in Zurich.
We said "Good-bye" at the train station—
it was to be a "Good-bye" for two years
as he was called back to the United States.
Love letters crossed the Atlantic Ocean
but over the distance his love faded.
He got engaged
I got engaged
each to another
both engagements were broken—
He came back to Germany
and love was even "lovelier
the second time around."
I came to the States to study
we got engaged
we married
I left my family, my friends,
my country behind.
We were happy.
Over the years our love grew deeper
even when life got complex,
and it lasted.

Later Years

"We have changed," I say—
"It's nature's way!" you reply,
"did you think our youthful passion
would always stay that way?"

"You are right," I agree—
"When your hands touch me,
when my hands touch you
the fire is gone!"

The old emotions
cannot be called up again—
Our terms of endearment
now evoke a different thrill!

Time flies and flies,
has robbed us of our youth
but not of our steadfast love,
a love still so sweet
it remains our ally the future to meet.

"Dusty"

Who hurt you so, my foundling cat,
that each new person approaching,
each unexpected movement or sound
is such a threat?
You're trying to trust me, I can tell,
but each loud noise seems to put you in hell!
You run for your bed
wait to be reassured, to be pet.

You have learned my language better
than I have mastered yours,
commands like "come here!", "hop!", "no no!"
you have down pat, my scaredy-cat.
Your "meow in!", "meow out!", "meow food!"
I comprehend,
but your drawn out wailing attempts to communicate
I have not managed to validate.
I know you don't think me so terrific
when I ask you to be more specific!

You were de-clawed on all fours,
is that why you're so leery of people
and fear we are all really evil?
When strangers approach you run for cover
afraid one might come near, might hover.
Well, I'm not one of the bad kind,
learn that with your suspicious mind!

The vet said I could leave you for adoption
I do not want to consider that option—
you have suffered enough!
Though you continue to frustrate me
in time I can win you over, you'll see!
Then you'll no longer run from me,
you'll run to me!

A Happy Anniversary

Fifty years we've been together,
and—we've been apart.
Love has kept us in each other's heart
in calm and in stormy weather.

Did we choose wisely?
Did we choose well?
Most years were heaven,
some have been—oh well!

Oh well, we did say: "For better or for worse"—
We've had our share of each:
the heartaches and the walks on the beach,
and so let's stay our future's course!

For many years we knew no tears
but those of joy!
Times of grief
were few, and brief.

Now that the sun has set on our youth
let's hold hands a little longer
as we continue to walk in step,
while our hearts beat as one
and our love lingers on.

You, My Heart

I loved you when we were young,
I love you still, no even more
than all the years we shared before

I could never think you out of my life
it's been such a joy being your wife!
Any time you are away from me
 I yearn for your return

If some of my days are ever bad
with you by my side
it's never long that I am sad
you, My Heart, have all of my heart!

In the Blink of an Eye

"Your husband is dead"
to me in the hospital they said.
"Your husband is dead!"
My God, no! How can it be?
He'd promised never to leave me!

They take me to him
He's so pale, so still—
"Please be in a place where I can find you!"
in his ear I pray,
then, sobbing, I kiss his beloved lips "Good-bye,"
leave him to be cremated
as some day so will be I.

Dazed I start up the car,
It's to take me back to "our home"
alone—
now forever so alone!

The day has barely begun,
We had such plans on what we'd do—
It's all changed, my Beloved, without you!
Never again will I share these rooms with you,
never again our bed, so filled with love!
Oh, God, please grant me mercy from above!

Loss

You died—
I've lost you
so soon, too soon!
You took my heart with you
I'm left an empty shell
a body that can never be well!

I need your arms,
your loving touch,
my Sweetheart, I miss you so much!
My love will not die
why must I still live, why?

Without you, my Beloved,
daily routine cannot fulfill my life—
I am still your wife
but happy memories do not comfort me,
they are not reality, just images I see.

When I die our spirits will combine,
I'll see you then
they say—
Let it be true, I pray!

What Next?

Our cat is looking for you,
walks from room to room meowing,
misses his favorite lap—yours!
I'm weeping as I pet him:
"I'm so sorry, cat,
now it's just you and me!"

Friends come by—they care, I know,
but time drags on,
and when they go
the silence crushes me,
pain engulfs me—
I do not want to be "free"!

There are no words to express my grief
I try to pray—
but God seems so far away!
Will He help me still
when I've neglected Him so?
Please, God, show me a path where I can go!

Mortally Wounded

I feel like a wounded animal
that should be put out of its misery
as anyone can see!

Who is willing to give me the coup de grace?
A hunter would!
You think you could?

My mirror reflects a face
so wan, so drawn!
Can this really be me?

Your death left me empty—
My future without you, my Beloved, I cannot see!
Please God, lead me on, have mercy on me!

Be Strong

"You can do this," to me they say,
"You're strong and competent," they say—
Yes, yes, I know!
But why should I make the effort,
Why?

The phone rings off the hook!
So many people want to share my grief
because you, my Beloved, are gone!
They all mean so well
but no one can grasp my private hell!

Friends bring by flowers,
so many flowers—
They do not help me pass
the lonely hours.

I can't sleep—
there are so many tears to weep.
The night is dreary,
I get up weary
to face life without you now—
if only someone could tell me how!

Hurting Still

Eight weeks ago today we saw a movie,
had a romantic dinner,
went to bed.
In the morning you were dead—
and now I wish I too were dead!

The pain is not subsiding
it's constantly there
submerged
but ready to erupt with each memory,
and memories are everywhere!

At night a fitful sleep,
in the morning I weep—
So quiet the house!
There were times I complained when you swore,
would that you could be here
to swear some more!

So many thoughts go through my head
but one stays faithful:
I wish, my Dearest, I too were dead!

Wondering

"Your husband was not your raison d'être"
the therapist said to me,
how I wish I could agree!

I know my Beloved is dead,
I know my life needs changed direction
something that could give me new satisfaction.
"Seek and ye shall find!"
I must pass this along to my mind!

No more hugs from my Beloved
No more impromptu dances in our living room—
How do I live a life that now holds so much gloom?
When will this feeling of loss and loneliness end?
Could there be a raison d'être,
a new reason for my being waiting around the bend?

Day after Day

There were times, day after day, I made you laugh,
really laugh
and we would both feel good!
There were times I made you angry
and spoiled your happy mood.

The mind calls up memories
some funny, some tender, some sad—
There was the time your loud sneeze
shocked the cat right off the bed
who didn't seem to understand
how suddenly he was on the floor
yanked out of his dreams of a moment before—
Oh, how we laughed!

There were times you held me
when nightmares struck,
times when for your contests
I always wished you good luck!
Whatever life brought our way
we faced it together, day after day!

View from the Kitchen Window

The view from the kitchen window is perfect:
the roses bloom as lovely as ever,
the clematis has joined the buttercups,
I mow the little courtyard
as I always have—
Nothing has changed,
yet everything is changed!
You're no longer here to see,
and I'm different without you!

One Hand Clapping

Spring is here again, but you are not!
How you loved the blooming shrubs and roses,
and cardinals and pretty birds
whose names you did not always know!
How often you'd call to me:
"Come quickly, Herzchen, this one you must see!"
How we savored the beauty of spring
and fall
and the white Christmases
unencumbered by any thought
that we might not forever be together
in all kinds of weather—

I want to applaud the new spring
in all its glory
but now alone
it feels like one hand clapping—
the harmony is gone!

I Want to Live Again

I look at people around me—they are alive,
I feel that I am not!
"It's too soon, don't expect too much of yourself,
he hasn't been gone that long" people say to me.
Why does it seem like an eternity?

If the salt were to lose its saltiness
Could it be restored?
How does one infuse life
into a "dead person walking"?

In church we sing:
"Trust and obey!"
but God's help is taking so long
to come my way.

I want to leave this lifeless state
I want to embrace a brand new fate!
Knowing that life is precious
I want to live again!

Moments Remembered

This is the time in the evening
when the phone would ring
and it would be you:
"Just checking in to see how you are doing,"
and briefly we would chat
about this and that.

Or, instead of walking through the door
you might call once more:
"I'm sorry, I'm running late, My Sweet,
don't wait up, go on to sleep!"
I miss those loving evening calls,
my heart is heavy, and I weep.

When I die I want you to stand at Heaven's door
your arms open for me, singing
as you have done so many times before:
"Embrace me, My Sweet Embraceable You"
and I'd fly into your arms to be
your "Irreplaceable You" forevermore!

I Sold Your Car

I sold your car!
Now there's another empty space
where you used to fit into my life.

In the garage my car stands alone,
her nightly companion is gone—
My car does not feel my loss, my pain
it responds to my control
in sunshine and rain—
Lucky car!

Sometimes you sat beside me,
now I drive alone
you, My Beloved, are gone—
yet my heart remembers happiness,
embraces, bliss,
your smile, your kiss
with such intensity
as though all were still reality.
Lucky me!

Yearning

I yearn for the place of perfect tranquility,
yearn to accept my fate with serenity,
yearn to be free of envy, hate or need to blame
and look at life with equanimity,
when I can see in my solitude
a blessing from God above
and know I'll never be without His love!

I Walk Alone

The sky is blue
tufts of white clouds hang suspended
the air is calm
the day has ended
the moon is waiting for the night
to cover the earth with its light.

The familiar path I now walk without you
but my thoughts are all about you
the memories of so many happy years
do not deserve to be bathed in tears,
you died, the wonder of our love will not,
not ever—no never!

I don't need to look at our forget-me-nots
to keep you in my heart
and I know it's not forever
that you and I will be apart.

Life Goes On

I want to write a happy poem
about the warming sun,
I want to describe your favorite bush, my Love,
but it refuses to bloom!
I want to write about our little wren
returning to his house,
but it hangs empty!
Could he not endure life
when last summer he lost his wife?
His chirping for a new mate
apparently came too late—
but life goes on!

The little bird's fate leaves me sad
and I want so much to feel glad!
I try to sing a new song, my Dearest,
without you,
not just about you!
I want to overcome my pain!
Am I doomed to try in vain?
No, I know that life goes on!

How Do I Miss You

How do I miss you
let me count the ways:
"I miss you in the morning sun
and when the day is done,"
I miss you when the lilacs bloom,
I miss you when thunder looms,
and when the days get colder
I miss the warmth of your shoulder;
I miss your hand in mine in prayer,
the many ways we were together;
I miss your kiss
our married bliss
your loving eyes searching for me,
your joy in how our days turned out to be;
I miss our sharing,
your caring,
our walks together
in all kinds of weather;
I miss your laughter
when I said something stupid,
clearly we were never far from Cupid!

Songs and poems expressed my feelings before—
I only know: I miss all of you forever more!

The Way We Were

We could laugh at the weather
snow, storm and ice
they did not matter:
we were together!
What strength we drew from each other
while the joys of May turned into December
and summer flowers no longer bloomed
like glowing amber!

When the cold drove the birds away
to follow the sun
we would stay—
we'd make it through the dreary days
wait for the New Year to be born
trusting our love to keep us warm.

Lived, Loved, Lost

Mirror, mirror on the wall:
Wasn't I one of the prettiest of them all?
How cruel you are to now let me see a face
that no longer shows beauty and inner peace!
Can this really be me?
The once so tiny laugh lines
have turned into deep furrows
sculpted by so many of life's sorrows,
by the tears when at times you took your love away,
and when you died, more grew so deep
as my nights were spent grieving with little sleep—

My eyes have lost their sparkle
my eyelids droop,
is it to shut out a world so full of trouble?
Gone, all that once I treasured
and found so worth living for, so memorable,
gone my youthful energy, your love, my happiness
replaced by painful loneliness—
In the blink of an eye
life has passed me by!

But wait! Mightn't I still leave the world a better place?
All I have to do is try!

Never to Know Each Other

We speak half truths,
never bare our soul
which is covered by the shell of our body
like the coral at the bottom of the sea
hidden by the waters washing over it.

Fearing our fragile strings of friendship, of love
might break
if the risk of openness we take
we stay in our cocoon,
we play it safe!

Who of us is strong enough
to face rejection
when unconditional love
might not be given to imperfection?

Am I Really Old Now?

"When you enter a room people notice you,"
a young friend once said to me—
Wasn't that just a season ago?
I've checked it out and I find
it is no longer so!
I didn't need to be noticed back then,
for then I had my own man,
but he is gone,
I am alone!

Now that I'm in my twilight years
people don't give me a glance
don't find me noteworthy any more.
Why does that hurt so?
I once had it all
now I'm left with only memories to recall.

Please don't write me off!
Couldn't you please just not ignore me?
I know something that youth
as yet doesn't know:
One day you too will be old
but I won't be around to say:
"I told you so!"

Senseless Hurts

I tease you
you don't smile,
I get sarcastic
you shut down.
I've broken the bridge
that could bring us closer—
Insecurity makes me do stupid things!
Your silence hurts me,
I want to hurt back
we sulk
until we go to bed.
"Don't ever go to bed mad!"
people have often said—
Good advice,
but to us given in vain,
we ignore it
and suffer the pain!

Let's Not Do It!

I know you lost your wife
I lost my husband too.
Yes, we're both lonely
but there is no quick fix
so let's not put "getting intimate"
into the mix!
Please comprehend:
I can be no more
than just your friend!

Answers, Please!

Why is it life races by so fast?
Why is it our bliss on earth doesn't last?
Wasn't it just yesterday
the future lay before us?
We danced the nights away
in Oslo, Warsaw, Madrid, Prague,
sipped champagne on ships
as we sailed to foreign shores
found time for friends, family
studied hard, had a career
built our house, made love
and loved without a care.

We were a team, you and I,
why did it have to end?
Why?
What unfriendly fairy
waved her magic wand
and made it all disappear—too soon—
at her command?
Answers, please!

Man Buying Flowers

The man in the store is buying flowers—
For his wife?
For his girlfriend?
Envy gnaws at my heart!
I know that isn't fair,
for over fifty years
of bouquets I got more than my share—
It's not the flowers I miss
but the loving man
who gave them to me
with a kiss.

To Be Loved Again

Would that I could be loved again
by a man so kind and true
that I would want his hand in mine
to cherish each other come rain or shine!

I'm in the autumn of my life,
am I too bold to hope
a good man might still want me by his side?
What a miracle that would be!
If only you could grant it, Lord,
new joy in my life I might see.

The house is so still;
I sit alone,
not even the sound of the telephone—
The rose outside my window stands tall
swaying gently in the wind
that will make its petals fall.
So short its glory,
so short everyone's story—

Life and love race by so fast!
We grasp at happiness
knowing it won't last,
yet we try and try—
hope is the reason why!

An Unexpected Friend

I have a new friend!
I didn't think she could ever be
a true friend to me since she'd been close
to a person who'd hurt me so seriously.

Now I know that the improbable can happen!
She's bringing joy into my life,
a life that had been so bleak since my Beloved died
and without him I couldn't seem to find
a reason to go on living—

She is so giving
So caring
So nourishing
Encouraging
She listens when I need to vent—
How could I not be grateful
for such a friend!

Invitation to a Party

Should I go—alone?
Perhaps reconnect?
I go.
Excited people
Friends
Colleagues
Chatter
Laughter
Hugs
Glad you could make it!
I just heard—I'm so sorry!
Moving to the buffet
Sitting down
Eating
Muffled exchanges
Mingling
Planning any trips?
Not this year—
So good to see you!
You too!
How are you doing?
Fine, just fine!
Back from your trip already?
Planned it that way so I could see you!
Shouldn't have!
Why not?
My question: Why?
Regular coffee? Yes fine!
Great fashion show coming up,
At a country club!
Sounds fine
Will you come?

Maybe—call me, I'll see!
So much superficiality here,
Might deeper connections follow?
Leaving already?
Must go—get home!
Home?
Silent House.

The Empty Chair

Life isn't fair!
Next to me stands the empty chair
where you, my Beloved, would sit and share
evening time with me.
But you are gone,
I sit alone!

I keep looking at that chair
knowing you can no longer be there—
I still watch "our" program on TV,
make a comment,
turn to you to see if you agree,
the chair is empty and sadness grips me!

How I wish we could go on sharing,
you by my side, loving and caring!
Your spirit is enshrined in my heart
but your spirit can't hug,
joke, comfort me—
Without you I'm not really me!

I'm surfing the channels now
not enjoying what I see—
But wait! There are the Smothers Brothers
who came on the air just now!
We would have laughed in unison
at their hilarious presentations—

Laughing alone is bittersweet!

What Did You Love?

When you said: "I love you!"
did you love what you could see
or did you look more deeply,
did you love all of me—
imperfect me?

Guidelines for Life

God gave us commandments to obey
and a free will to help us not to stray.

We can choose to spread love or pain,
hope our struggles won't be in vain,
as we search for wisdom along the way
to guide us through life, come what may.

One Last Kiss

Thank you, Sweetheart, for leaving one last kiss
on the rim of your wine glass for me to see,
on a glass which you would always use
when dining without me!
You'd claim the "better" glasses would be wasted on you,
they should be kept safe just for us two.

Thank you for not washing that glass so perfectly,
it preserved the shape of your mouth so clearly!
I drank your kiss—the wine I didn't miss!

First Christmas without You, My Love

The Christmas candle flickers
 burned down to half its size
My eyes are focused on it
willing it to conjure up the spirit of Christmas in me,
to recapture the memory of our last Christmas together!
I fail—
I sit alone,
No more shared joy—that's all over now!

What a difference the last year has made!
I have lived it without you since you died—
Lived it?
The passing time has carried me along,
My heart aches for the lost joys of years shared
that can nevermore be—
I try to hum a familiar Christmas tune
 but can't feel its message!
Dare I look to next year with hope?

The Nutty Squirrel

The little squirrel is digging ferociously
by the rose bush outside my living room window.
Dirt is flying up, he's digging deeper and deeper,
now his head is underground!

Do you really remember burying "it" right there?
You won't find "it"!
How many times have I seen your kind digging in vain!
But wait! What's that?
He's out of the hole and there's a big black walnut
in his mouth.

I'm impressed!
Now let me see you crack the shell!
Oh no! He's digging another hole under the pine tree
and burying it again!
Are you nuts, putting that nut back in the ground?

No one must know he's buried something there!
Carefully his little paws move dirt and leaves
back over the hole.
Good! No one will find it!
But what to do for food?
That crab apple tree over there still has some apples.

It's a good thing claws can dig and help climb trees, too!

The Christmas Tree

The little girl in the hospital is so sick!
Not a good time to be sick and away from home!
"Aaah!" she marvels as she sees me brought into the room.
Her eyes sparkle,
she looks at me in awe!

Yes, I look glorious
decked out in my Christmas finery
All my branches gleam
like bracelets on a beautiful woman's arms
Golden garlands encircle me
and the tinsel glitters.

My fresh pine-tree fragrance fills the room!
I was sad when they cut me down
to be a Christmas tree
but now I'm glad!
I have done my best deed:
brought joy to a sick child's heart!

A Summer's Eve Remembered

Dinner is ready,
It would be nice if you'd come home now!
We'll eat on the patio,
The balmy air entices.

I step out on our driveway
Great! There's your Saab turning the corner
You see me standing there
Slow the car, smile at me

I clap my hands: perfect timing!
"Put your car in the garage and join me!"
You come,
Kiss me.

We sit down to eat, chat, relax,
 Linger until darkness falls—
A lovely evening, like so many we have enjoyed
And there'll be more to come!

I'm day-dreaming—
There can't be another such evening:
You died!
It hurts too much to sit here alone.

Pure As the Driven Snow

Earth wears a blanket of snow
in the purest white
like a virgin's wedding gown
ready for the groom.
Snow flakes bless the waiting bride.

Who will the bridegroom be?
Spring would make the perfect mate!
Earth would melt in his warm arms
give up her gown
ready for seed to be sewn
that in her new life may grow.

It's good to be earth!

Beyond

When at last my heart stops beating
and my spirit enters the place beyond
it's not just my body I shall leave behind
but all earthly feelings as well:
desire
passion
love
anger
euphoria
hurts
failures
disappointments
sorrows

Joys of a heavenly nature
await me in the beyond
where with the spirits of loved ones
I can form a new bond.
Hatred, envy, jealousy, distrust
will no longer weigh me down
where my life in serenity will go on

To my Heavenly Father I pray:
Take each phase of my life in your hands
and when here on earth it ends
please lead me to the Promised Land!

Hard Dates without You

Valentine's Day
Easter
My birthday
Our wedding anniversary
Your birthday
Thanksgiving
Christmas
New Year's Day

For the first time without you!
I made it through these special days
Thank you, Lord!

Next to come:
The first anniversary of your death—
Will that day be any harder than each day?
Will my pain ever diminish?

Now I know the answer:
My pain's intact
though slightly cracked,
ever so slightly!

Joy must step lightly
but persistently into that crack,
widen it
until pain is pushed aside.

My Sweetheart

There's your empty hobby room—
you'll no longer create in it, my Sweetheart,
that chapter is closed!

When will I write the final chapter on my grief?
When will I go to bed
and no longer feel the sting
of the empty space beside me?

When will I wake up grateful to be alive
and no longer miss your "Good Morning!" kiss?
When will the road I sadly walk without you
become the path I can joyfully walk alone?

God has sustained me every step of my way
but His is the spirit's touch
not the comfort of your human arms
I loved so much!

There can be no closing chapter on our shared life!

Night into Morning

I go to bed
pull the cover over my head
pretend I'm dead.
Pretend?
All through the night I am dead!

Morning comes
I throw the cover back—
A new day to fill!
What a thrill it could be,
it's all up to me!

"Good morning, my cat!"
"Meow" you say,
 just that, just "meow"?
Could you please make it a "meow-we"?
Think it over, my little house rover!

A Very Special Bracelet

Today I'm wearing that gold bracelet again,
it is heavy and has a beautiful design
and for now I can call it mine.

It was on my mother's wrist
when she and my father had come to see me here,
the bracelet a gift to their only child
who had married a foreigner
so far away from home—
they needed to know
if any good of it had come.

Always this bracelet evokes memories of my mother.
It remains very dear to me since it graced her wrist,
a wrist that had been attached to such a loving hand!
My sweet mother is long gone
yet this bracelet, an artist's creation, lives on!

After I too shall have turned to ashes
another woman will wear it,
and then another—
The bracelet cannot pass along stories
about the women to whom it brought joy
an inanimate object, it will "live" on
long after all who admired its beauty
will from this earth have gone.

Cat's "Happy Birthday" to a Dear Friend

Being of the "advanced species" that we cats are
we grow our own fur—the best of any by far!
Much as we would like to share
with our dear mamas some of our hair
they just brush it off
and scoff!

Now then, if we want humans to be warm in style
We've got to resort to some feline wile,
so my mama and I collected some pennies
and paid for a fur for you, Dear Friend.

When my mama is away
you feed me every day!
It's only fair that in her present to you
as best as I can I share!

North to South

Can I do this by myself:
Fly from the wintery North
to the summery South?
Yes, I can!

Warm sun embraces my bare arms and legs,
balmy sea breeze tousles my hair,
two small burrowing owls watch me
as I pass by their lair
interested, but unafraid they don't hide.

It's a treat to walk to the beach
where people bake in the sun
and children romp having fun.

On the pier I sit and gaze at the calming water—
Oh, that poor pelican must be hurt
he doesn't seem to fly right
diving head first clumsily into the sea.

But look: up comes his beak
and he is swallowing his catch!
He knew what he was doing
and dives for fish again and again
while another pelican rests on a pole
apparently filled with his catch of the day.

I turn to the shore and am treated to more:
two beautiful white pelicans are landing there
ever so gracefully,
then fly off again to further explore the shore.

A big tree on the beach holds a flock of tiny
multi-colored parakeets chirping merrily.
People stare up at them, try to take their picture
as they fly from branch to branch
too fast, alas!

There will be dolphins to watch, I am told,
but at a different time of day and place.
I'll be there, I can wait—
Observing nature is my fun in the sun.

"Life Is But a Dream"

I look at the hundreds of pictures
of you and me, friends and family
but mostly pictures of you and me
happy, laughing, goofy snap shots
spanning the 50+ years we spent together:
Our life.

That was our life, the pictures say
but try as I may
this past reality escapes me
like a dream that vanishes in the morning.
Because you died so suddenly without warning
it altered my state of reality.
Painful conflicts will forever remain unresolved
now that you are gone.

After a time of mourning, moments of grief still pop up
triggered by so many memories,
by all the objects in our house we selected together,
by missing your face and loving hands
joined with mine across the breakfast table
as we said grace in thanks for each new day.

Though the life as I knew it with you
has come to a stop
the world around me has not.
The sun still shines, the rains still fall
nurturing new life in the spring.
I want to begin my new "spring of life" too!
With God's help, I trust, I can make it come true.

Sunday

If this is the day the Lord has made
I wish he'd done better!
It's cold and blustery
and there's not a speck of sun
no, this day is no fun!

I'd like to go for a walk,
call up a friend, have a talk,
forget about my fickle lover
he's gone, that's that,
it's over, you restless rover!

Caution seems to keep my friends
from answering the phone,
I could be a telemarketer
they call on any day, at any hour
it makes us all quite sour!

A flash of red on the tree outside:
a cardinal taking a rest.
Now there's a welcome sight to see,
thank you, little bird, you are the day's best!
You've taken the focus away
from self-centered me.

Rubber Bands

I'm playing with a rubber band
stretch it, twist it, wind it around my finger,
my wrist, snap it back against my hand—ouch!
I try to shoot little paper balls into the basket
miss—
Not much fun this!

Rubber bands are meant for more serious tasks:
you can stretch them over bundles of paper
and they hold them together
you can use them over and over
until they become brittle
or pop when stretched beyond their breaking point.

Would that we could learn from the little rubber bands!
Test, twist, stretch a relationship too far
and you split it apart.
Would that a little rubber band could hold lovers together
but we're on our own there—
sometimes we snap back
and sometimes we break.

Then and Now

The house is so still,
I sit here alone
now that you are gone—
Is it God's will
that for mistakes in our marriage
I must atone alone?

If only I had listened more
accepted more
forgiven more
encouraged more
grasped chances for closeness more!

"Don't look back with regrets," friends say,
"he wasn't blameless either!"
 Far from it, I know!
Then why is my pain so slow to go?
The shared happiness doesn't cancel it out!

We made love on this carpet,
held each other on that couch,
sat talking on those chairs,
danced to Latin rhythms we couldn't resist,
and years ago even enjoyed doing the Twist.

You found the stunning redwood table,
I the marble sculpture on it
The music cabinet we selected together,
and the pictures on the wall,
and the clocks
that now tic-toc in this silent room.

I miss you so much!
I loved you so much!
Did you love me as much?

Outside the sun is shining,
I must stop repining!

My Love

He lifts me in the air in joyful playfulness—I shriek with surprised delight: "No, no! Put me down, you'll hurt your back!" He is my husband, 6'1" tall, 190 lbs, young, strong, handsome—and he loves me. "Bestes" he calls me, honoring my German background, "Herzi" and "Suesser" are the loving terms I bestow on him. We have been married for 25 years and we love each other!

Fast forward to 25 years later. The love is still there, but exuberant moments have become rare. His back now hurts, he has survived brain surgery which left him battling seizures for the rest of his life. I need to watch him that he doesn't forget to take his pills because if he does he has seizures and they can kill. He hates taking the medication and takes the lowest possible dose though he knows that is dangerous, but he doesn't want to feel drowsy. "They screwed up my brain!" he complains. "No, Dear, they saved your life!" I counter. "I never promised you a rose garden," that old hit tune comes to my mind. We all know that life isn't fair but when that truth hits, it hits hard!

My clinical psychologist therapist husband has helped so many people lead better lives, but how can he help himself? His second book on model airplanes is in the making. All his spare time is given to his hobby: designing, building and flying his airplanes. Trophies won in airplane competitions cover two shelves in our house and there are plaques on the wall. It is harder now to build. Sometimes things get put together wrong, building takes so much time because arthritic fingers are no longer nimble. Frustration erupts in anger. Yet there is still his faith to pull him through. A deeply spiritual human being, he sees himself joining God's creative force after death.

And now he has gone home to God! An acute seizure ended his life suddenly and quickly. So much love, creativity, accomplishment, helpfulness is gone. What a waste! Or is it? He left a broad path behind in all the lives he touched! My love-filled life has ended with his. My living loving husband I could never have lifted off the ground, but the five pounds of his ashes are no problem for me at all. I'll keep him with our roses which he loved so much—I'll keep him close to me.

Rest in peace, my Beloved!

Not for Me

"They're writing songs of love, but not for me"—
so sings Ella Fitzgerald.

Love songs now make me sad!
You are gone, and with you so is your love
and my loving you,
our life, our purpose, our future together!
I feel so alone and so very lonely.

Spring is here again,
and all of nature returns to life,
why can nature come back
but a beloved person cannot?
Forever now apart
all I can do is keep you in my heart.

Imperfect Joy

"Geteilte Freude ist doppelte Freude" (German wisdom)
It means "joy shared is joy doubled."

The day is too picture-perfect to savor alone!
A sea of flowers surrounds the patio—
roses, clematis, buttercups, sweet rockets,
foxglove, daisies, cornflowers, campions,
geraniums, petunias, gaillardias—oh, so many more
too numerous to name!

It seems as though after cold and stormy rainy days
nature has burst out of prison
releasing its stored-up magnificence
in generous abundance.
 Yellow finches are taking a dip in the bird bath,
refreshed, they fly off, letting a blue jay have its turn.

The sun shines blessing on nature's splendor,
a gentle warm breeze seduces to dreaming—
Could this day be any more perfect?
Yes, if shared with a beloved person!

Wishing

I wish that you could be
The new man in my life
You—loyal, dependable, faithful, committed
The very reasons why you can't ever be
That man for me.

Still, I can wish!

Be Careful What You Pray For!
A Very Short Story

Mommy! Mommy! is a call I'll never hear from a child of mine. Two neighboring women and five small children just walked by on the road, two more children skipped happily along in a different direction. A school bus had just dropped them off, and some of them started running home ahead of their mothers, but then one of them urgently needed her mom. No one had seen me sitting on the patio on the first wonderfully warm spring day of the year, sitting here alone now, since my husband died.

"Be careful what you pray for," they say, "you might get it!" Well I did! Get it, I mean. A willowy maiden, I'd stand in front of a mirror asking God to always let me be slim (He did), to make my budding breasts just a little bit bigger (He did!), and to never ever let me become pregnant (this He granted also).

I grew up and became very attractive to men of varying ages. I was loved by many—a few I even loved back, two in particular: one I married, the other one I should have. The one I married was as self-centered as was I. He wanted no children either, although for a time we actually tried to get me pregnant—without success.

After early years of infatuation, his adoring me, putting me on a pedestal with pride wore off, and we disappointed each other. He "woke up," needed and looked elsewhere for "more" than I could give, and my life became a bore. Even so, we stayed married for over fifty years, filled with joy and tears. I had a lot, but missed out on more.

The other one, the one I did not marry, would have remained faithful to me, loved me more committedly. I could have loved him back equally—actually I do! We still love each other from a great distance, sign our letters "Love, as ever."

Do I have regrets? Oh yes! I prayed for the wrong things, prayed for external beauty which can't last—and got it! No, "Mommy! Mommy!" is a cry I will never hear from a child of mine! I should have prayed for fulfillment and love, lasting love!

When Breaks Happen

My glasses fell from my lap
I didn't see them fall
I stepped on them
broke the frame!
My best reading glasses!
What can I do?
To the rescue: Super Glue,
it will bond almost anything
make it stronger than ever before!

What's the super glue to mend
a broken relationship?
Only love, lots of love
and two people striving to come together
can heal the break,
and with a lot of patience,
forgiveness and understanding
the relationship might grow strong again.
Stronger than ever?
Sometimes—perhaps!

Traveling Alone

My travel documents arrived:
I'm going to Europe,
to Germany, the land of my birth
my first trip alone since you died.
Oh, I've made that trip without you before
but over the distance we'd connect
and I knew when I'd come back
you'd welcome me home with loving arms.
This trip will be different!

Am I ready for remembrances we shared,
for new joys?
Friends who care will still be there.
Will I be able to mean it
when I answer "Fine!" to "How are you?"
Will it hurt to return home alone?
In our love-filled life time was so short!
Now, unloved, it seems endless.

Autumn Dance of the Leaves

Dance with me!
I'm ash
you're birch
together we'd be quite a smash!
Catch me as I pirouette
watch the water puddle
don't get wet
or you'll no longer fly
high in the sky!

It hurt to be torn from our mothers' arms
but now we're free
some more of the world to see
with the wind in our wings
over the church steeple we'll swing.
We cannot see what's on the other side
but as pilgrims we'll fly
until the wind gently sets us down
on Father Earth to die.

How Tall You Have Grown

Forty-five years ago we planted you,
a tiny 2' blue spruce tree,
on our newly acquired lot we planted you,
my husband and I, both young,
eager to add beauty to our home.

You flourished and grew and grew
gracing the corner of our house
for us to enjoy from two windows.
The birds and squirrels loved your shelter
and the pine cones, as you matured.

While the scotch pine we also planted
stretched its branches out wide
you kept growing upwards to the sky,
slim, tall, straight.
Throughout the cold and snowy winters
your needles never faded,
stayed a lovely blue-green.

Thank you for the joy you have given us,
and still give to me, now alone,
since my husband died.
You are the loyal Tannenbaum,
praised in song, so well-deserved!

Love's Power

"It's better to have loved and lost
than never to have loved at all"—
After the pain of losing you to death
comes the joy of remembering
all that can never be lost.

The love you gave me
remains enshrined in my heart!
Your love brought out the best in me
inspired me
made me strong to face life without fear
I can heal
find new joy.

I have loved you
and been loved by you in return,
that I could share my life with you
has been a gift and a blessing.
Love is stronger than grief—
"Thanks for the memories!"

Carpe Diem

Life is a poem of moments
like seconds that tick on quickly.
We try to hold on to happiness
but like our sorrows nothing lasts
not our failures
not our joys
not the missed opportunities
of our past.

When at last we get wise we realize
that each moment is our gift of being alive
to be lived without fear of tomorrow
or regret of yesterday
without fear of death,
that final moment of life—
for we know: this too shall pass!